Mastering Autofac
Advanced Dependency Injection for .NET Applications

Table of Contents

Chapter 1. Introduction

In a world where software complexity constantly increases, mastering Dependency Injection (DI) becomes an absolute necessity for any .NET developer. 'Mastering Autofac: Advanced Dependency Injection for .NET Applications' is a Special Report crafted meticulously for developers aiming to dive deep into the ocean that is Autofac, one of the most powerful tools for DI in the .NET galaxy. This comprehensively detailed document provides much-needed clarity on using Autofac to architect loosely-coupled and scalable applications with improved testability. Whether you're just dabbling with Dependency Injection or looking to engineer enterprise-level solutions, this report promises to be an invaluable companion, breaking down intricate concepts into easy-to-understand, practical examples. Immerse yourself in the potent combination of Autofac and .NET, and transform the way you design, develop, and maintain your software applications.

Chapter 2. Understanding Dependency Injection: The Basics

Dependency Injection (DI) is a crucial pattern that promotes loosely coupled and reusable components, setting the foundation for larger architectures such as Domain Driven Design, CQRS, Event Sourcing, and Unit of Work. Despite being quite simple in theory, it can become tricky and confusing when put to practical use.

Before diving further into the topic, let's begin with defining what Dependency Injection actually is.

According to Martin Fowler, "Dependency Injection is a 25-dollar term for a 5-cent concept." That '5-cent' concept is essentially all about removing the hard-coded dependencies and making it interchangeable.

2.1. What is Dependency Injection (DI)?

Dependency Injection is a software design pattern in which dependencies of an object are set by external means, typically through a constructor, property, or method call. DI's primary objective is to remove the dependency from the programming code to make systems more modular, more testable, and more maintainable.

Let's take a look at a scenario without Dependency Injection:

```
public class OrderService
{
```

```
        private IOrderDataAccess _orderDataAccess;

        public OrderService()
        {
            _orderDataAccess = new SqlOrderDataAccess();
        }

        public void ProcessOrder(Order order)
        {
            _orderDataAccess.Save(order);
        }
    }
```

In this example, the OrderService depends on SqlOrderDataAccess, because it's hard-coded within the class. If the data source changes, the OrderService class has to be rewritten.

In contrast, if Dependency Injection was used:

```
public class OrderService
{
    private IOrderDataAccess _orderDataAccess;

    public OrderService(IOrderDataAccess
orderDataAccess)
    {
        _orderDataAccess = orderDataAccess;
    }

    public void ProcessOrder(Order order)
    {
        _orderDataAccess.Save(order);
    }
}
```

In the improved example, `OrderService` doesn't care if the data is saved in SQL, NoSQL, or in-memory; it's abstracted away. This way, the dependencies are decoupled, making the code more modular and testable.

2.2. Understanding DI Components

A dependency injection framework involves three key components: Service, Client, and Injector.

1. *Service:* This is the object being used by the client.
2. *Client:* This is the object that requires the dependency.
3. *Injector/Container:* This object is responsible for injecting the service into the client.

Let's understand the process with an analogical example. Assume you are constructing a house (the Client). The house needs modules or rooms (the Services) like a kitchen, a bedroom, and a bathroom. Now, instead of building these rooms by yourself, you hire a contractor (the Injector). The contractor finds the required modules and inserts them into your house efficiently and effectively.

2.3. Types of Dependency Injection

There are three main types of Dependency Injection: Constructor Injection, Property Injection, and Method Injection.

1. *Constructor Injection:* This is the most popular form of dependency injection where the Injector passes the dependencies through the constructor of the client. A strong point of this approach is that it leaves your objects in a usable state after construction.
2. *Property Injection:* Also known as "Setter Injection", Property Injection introduces dependencies by creating public setter

properties in the client class which the Injector uses to set the appropriate dependency. While this also allows DI, it can lead to half-initialized objects.

3. *Method Injection:* In this approach, the Injector uses a public method to set dependencies. This way of injection is most helpful when a class introduces a method where it needs a service.

As a best practice, use constructor injection when the client can't perform its responsibilities without the dependency, and use property injection when the dependency is actually optional.

2.4. Benefits of Dependency Injection

While developing software, Dependency Injection provides several benefits:

1. *Reduced Coupling:* The client is not tightly bound with the service anymore, leading to loose coupling.

2. *Enhanced Testability:* With dependencies injectable, mocking becomes notably easier, enabling unit tests.

3. *Increased Readability:* It's easier to understand and follow the program flow as dependencies aren't hidden anymore.

4. *Improved Maintainability:* With loosely coupled components, any changes made to one component doesn't affect the others.

Dependency Injection might seem complicated at first, but once mastered, it significantly improves the scalability and testability of your .NET Applications.

In the next section, we will dive into Autofac, an addictive Inversion of Control container for .NET that simplifies the way you implement and work with Dependency Injection.

Chapter 3. Autofac: A Comprehensive Introduction

Autofac has emerged as an indispensable tool for Dependency Injection (DI) in the .NET ecosystem, thanks to its power and scalability. Offering flexibility and enabling changes without a total overhaul of the codebase, Autofac has proven itself indispensable for designing robust .NET applications. This chapter provides an exhaustive and comprehensive introduction to Autofac with illustrative examples for easy understanding.

3.1. Getting Started with Autofac

Autofac is an Inversion of Control (IoC) container used for DI in .NET applications. It helps developers manage and control the dependencies in their applications by enabling them to easily decouple components and services. The Autofac NuGet package can be effortlessly integrated into any .NET application to commence the implementation of DI.

To start with, the Autofac package can be installed using the Package Manager Console of Visual Studio with the following command: `Install-Package Autofac`.

Once the package is installed, the first step involves defining a container and configuring it to use Autofac. This can be achieved by creating an instance of `ContainerBuilder` and then adding components through different registration methods. Here's an simple snippet of how this can be done:

```
var builder = new ContainerBuilder();

builder.RegisterType<MyClass>();
```

The `RegisterType` method instructs Autofac to create a new instance of the class whenever a dependency needs to be resolved. The DI container then resolves these dependencies whenever a class is instantiated.

3.2. Understanding the Concepts of Autofac

Dependency Injection (DI) in Autofac is underpinned by three major entities: Components, Services, and Containers.

Components: These are the actual implementations that get registered with Autofac. They are typically .NET objects such as classes, instances or lambdas which are registered within the Autofac container.

Services: These represent the functionality exposed by a component. They can be interfaces, base classes, or even specific classes. Clients code against services, not components, ensuring decoupling.

Containers: They build mappings between services and the components that are to be used when such a service is required.

3.3. Registration Concepts

Autofac provides multiple methods to register components: - RegisterType - RegisterInstance - Register

Each of these methods have further sub-methods which can be used depending on the scenario and need of our application.

RegisterType is mostly used to register classes and services based on the type of the object. For example:

```
builder.RegisterType<DatabaseConnection>()

.As<IDatabaseConnection>()
```

```
.InstancePerLifetimeScope();
```

The 'Register' method can be used when more control over the object creation is required:

```
builder.Register(context ⇒ new Logs(context.Resolve<IConfig>()))

.As<ILogs>();
```

The RegisterInstance method is used when you want to register an existing instance of an object:

```
var output = new Output();

builder.RegisterInstance(output).As<IOutput>();
```

3.4. Component Lifetimes

When working with Autofac, it's crucial to understand the control over the lifetime and disposal of components. Autofac uses lifetimes to decide when to create new instances of the registered components. The default lifetime is per-dependency which means a new instance is created every time a dependency is requested. However, there are other built-in instance scopes or lifetimes: - Single Instance: One instance for the entire application lifecycle. - Instance Per Lifetime Scope: One instance per scope. - Instance Per Dependency: A unique instance each time.

Defining the lifetimes appropriately is very important for managing resources, avoiding leaks, and keeping data integrity intact.

3.5. Resolving Dependencies

After registering services and components, Autofac then resolves these dependencies when needed. For example, if a component 'A' needs 'B' to function, and if 'B' is registered in the container, Autofac can automatically resolve 'B' when 'A' is resolved.

```
var app = container.Resolve<MyClass>();
```

3.6. Layered Applications and Autofac Modules

When dealing with large-scale applications, these codes can be divided into layered assemblies. In such scenarios, Autofac uses modules to encapsulate all the registrations related to their layer in a single class. It ensures clean separation of concerns and a neat way to organize registrations.

3.7. Conclusion

Autofac is a comprehensive solution to implement dependency injection, with immense flexibility that paves the way for large scale, loosely coupled applications. Understanding and mastering it would truly empower any developer in their .NET journey, fortifying the scalability, testability and maintainability of their applications.

Chapter 4. Digging Deep into the Autofac Architecture

Before diving in, it's worth noting that what follows is a broad illustration of Autofac's architecture rather than an exhaustive guide. The real mastery requires dedication and hands-on experience.

Autofac is a powerful, extensible Dependency Injection container, built to efficiently resolve dependencies with .NET applications. It primarily focuses on constructor injection where dependencies are provided to a class through its constructor. The intrinsic components of Autofac are built around the core concepts of Register, Resolve, and Release. Now let's dissect these building blocks.

4.1. Deciphering the Basics

Autofac's operation revolves around the `Container`, which is the heart of the Autofac system - handling the registration and resolution of components. The `Container` is loaded with `Component Registrations`, each of which encapsulates a piece of object-making behavior as well as metadata about a component, such as its services and relationships with other components.

4.2. Untangling Component Registrations

Component Registrations serve a pivotal role in Autofac. A registration ties a logical Service to a Component that provides its implementation. Registrations are explicit - you need to specify which services a component provides. This can be achieved in multiple ways such as By Interface, by Name, by Metadata or via Delegate Factories.

4.3. Exploring Instance Scope

Objects in Autofac can be instance-per-dependency, single instance, instance-per-lifetime-scope, or instance-per-request. Each scope caters to specific needs pertinent to object reuse. The scope has significant performance and design implications, making it essential to choose wisely.

4.4. Unmasking Lifetime Scopes

These are Autofac's version of nested containers. A Lifetime Scope can be thought of as a cache or level of object scoping within a container. Effective utilization of Lifetime Scopes helps avoid issues such as leaking SingleInstance components and allows controlling deterministic disposal of Scoped services.

4.5. Dissecting Module Registrations

Autofac Modules encapsulate a set of related components for easy reusable packaging. They simplify your component registration code by encapsulating the group into a module. Internal services are usually specified in Modules to provide a layer of abstraction.

4.6. Comprehending Parameter Injection

One of the most powerful but commonly overlooked features in Autofac is the ability to wire up dependencies via Parameter Injection. Objects can be provided with other services via `constructor parameters`, `properties` (property injection), or `methods` (method injection).

4.7. Understanding Interceptors

Autofac allows for the interception of calls on the Concrete classes. This mechanism provides a way of automatically implementing cross-cutting concerns such as logging, caching, or exception handling without altering the actual implementation of the classes.

4.8. Teasing Apart Autofac Integration

Autofac offers seamless integration with a broad range of technologies like MVC, Web API, SignalR, among others. It eliminates the need for writing an extensive amount of plumbing code, making it easier to write neat and maintainable applications.

4.9. Examining Best Practices

Though Autofac offers immense flexibility, leveraging best practices can substantially enhance application robustness. The primary leadership revolves around thoughtful registration, careful structuring of Modules, minimalistic component lifetime, and wise utilization of Lifetime Scopes.

In the journey of mastering Autofac, understanding its essentials and deep-diving into specific elements is crucial. This deep dive into the Autofac architecture is an endeavor to empower you to harness the power of Autofac proficiently and leverage its capabilities to the fullest. Remember, the true power of a tool is in its efficient use, and this holds equally true for Autofac.

Resorting to Dependency Injection makes your applications code base less tightly coupled, more manageable, and testable. Armed with Autofac, your journey of writing maintainable .NET applications with DI just became easier.

Chapter 5. Lifetime Scopes and Instance Control in Autofac

The concept of lifetime and instance scopes in Autofac plays a crucial role in the management of resources within your applications. Understanding its intricacies in detail empowers you to construct more durable and scalable software.

5.1. Understanding Lifetime Scopes

Lifetime scopes control the duration of instances created by the container, much like a boundary for the instance - when it starts and when it ceases to exist. When you request an instance of a certain service, Autofac considers the lifetime scope. Aiming to provide developers with absolute control over instance management, Autofac offers several tools to earmark instance lifespan or 'lifetimes' to suit specific needs.

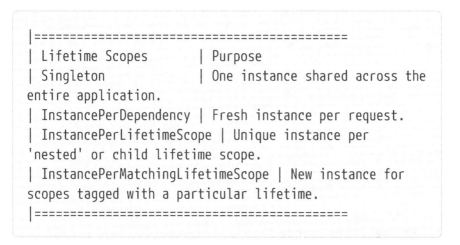

```
|================================================
| Lifetime Scopes        | Purpose
| Singleton              | One instance shared across the
entire application.
| InstancePerDependency  | Fresh instance per request.
| InstancePerLifetimeScope | Unique instance per
'nested' or child lifetime scope.
| InstancePerMatchingLifetimeScope | New instance for
scopes tagged with a particular lifetime.
|================================================
```

The lifetime scope functionality is on the component registration level to decide how instances for the particular component are shared.

For instance, for a Singleton scope,

```
public class Startup
{
    public void ConfigureContainer(ContainerBuilder builder)
    {

builder.RegisterType<MyComponent>().As<IMyComponent>().SingleInstance();
    }
}
```

This defines that MyComponent is a single instance - only one instance of MyComponent will be available in the whole application.

5.2. InstancePerDependency

InstancePerDependency creates a new instance every time when a service is being requested.

```
public class Startup
{
    public void ConfigureContainer(ContainerBuilder builder)
    {

builder.RegisterType<MyComponent>().As<IMyComponent>().InstancePerDependency();
    }
```

```
}
```

Every time a component depends on `IMyComponent`, Autofac will provide a new instance of `MyComponent`.

5.3. InstancePerLifetimeScope

InstancePerLifetimeScope shares instances within a same 'nested' or child lifetime scope. Different lifetime scopes will get different instances.

```
public class Startup
{
    public void ConfigureContainer(ContainerBuilder
builder)
    {

builder.RegisterType<MyComponent>().As<IMyComponent>().I
nstancePerLifetimeScope();
    }
}
```

5.4. InstancePerMatchingLifetimeScope

InstancePerMatchingLifetimeScope pulls a new instance for lifetime scopes that are tagged with a particular matching lifetime.

```
public class Startup
{
    public void ConfigureContainer(ContainerBuilder
builder)
```

```
    {

builder.RegisterType<MyComponent>().As<IMyComponent>().I
nstancePerMatchingLifetimeScope("myScope");
    }
}
```

5.5. Disposal of Resolved Services

Autofac keeps track of everything it resolves. When the lifetime scope of an object is over, Autofac automatically disposes of the instance and cleans up memory if it implements `IDisposable`. While the garbage collector takes care of non-managed resources in .NET, developers should still be diligent in cleaning up after themselves for managed resources and reduce the burden on the garbage collector to optimize applications. This level of control over instance duration, as well as cleanup, is yet another reason why mastering Autofac is an essential aspect of .NET programming.

5.6. Lifetime Scopes and Multithreading

When dealing with multithreaded applications, developers need to be conscious of the fact that lifetime scope isn't thread-safe. If two threads try to resolve services from the same lifetime scope concurrently, there could be potential problems. To overcome this, Autofac offers Thread Scope. With this, each thread has its own nested lifetime scope.

In conclusion, Autofac's Lifetime Scopes and Instance Control form a cornerstone of effective application design. Mastery of this can dramatically affect the efficiency, scalability, and reliability of your .NET Application. As we continue to delve into more complex and potent uses of Autofac and DI, the importance of these core concepts will be further illuminated. Join us in the next chapter where we discuss Integration of Autofac with various .NET architectures.

Chapter 6. Autofac in Action: Practical Examples

Let us begin by considering a simple .NET Core console application that uses Autofac for Dependency Injection. Following this, we will progress towards more complex scenarios to better comprehend and master the art of using Autofac.

6.1. Configuring Autofac in a Console Application

In a console application, the first thing you need to do is to install the Autofac NuGet package. Once installed, you can start configuring the Autofac container. The container essentially serves as a catalog of services that your application can use.

A typical Autofac container configuration looks something like this:

```
var builder = new ContainerBuilder();

builder.RegisterType<MyService>().As<IMyService>();

IContainer container = builder.Build();
```

In the above code, we've registered our service `MyService` against the interface `IMyService`. Henceforth, whenever any part of the application requests for `IMyService`, Autofac will provide an instance of `MyService`.

To resolve dependencies, you call the `Resolve` method on the container:

```
using(var scope = container.BeginLifetimeScope())
{
    var service = scope.Resolve<IMyService>();
}
```

Please note that resolving dependencies directly from the container is often considered an anti-pattern known as Service Locator. This is to be avoided in preference for using constructor injection.

6.2. Leveraging Constructor Injection

Suppose you have a class that depends on the IMyService interface, and you want Autofac to automatically inject it whenever it creates an instance of the dependent class.

```
public class Client
{
    private readonly IMyService _service;

    public Client(IMyService service)
    {
        _service = service;
    }
}
```

Here, the Client class has a dependency on IMyService. When the client is instantiated, Autofac will automatically provide an instance of IMyService (which, as per our registration, will be MyService), thus taking care of the injection part.

6.3. Assembling Applications with Modules

For complex applications that consist of multiple components or services, it would be cumbersome and counterproductive to have all registrations in a single place. This is where modules come in handy. Modules are basically a collection of registrations that can be bundled together.

Here is how you can define AutoFac modules:

```
public class ServiceModule : Module
{
    protected override void Load(ContainerBuilder
builder)
    {
        // Register all services

builder.RegisterType<MyService>().As<IMyService>();
    }
}
```

You can then load the module when configuring the container:

```
var builder = new ContainerBuilder();

builder.RegisterModule<ServiceModule>();

IContainer container = builder.Build();
```

6.4. Managing Object Lifetime

Autofac supports different lifetime scopes for services, allowing you to configure whether a new instance should be created every time a service is requested, or whether a single shared instance should be used.

InstancePerDependency() creates a new instance for every Resolve call, SingleInstance() shares the same instance every time, and InstancePerLifetimeScope() shares the same instance within a single lifetime scope, but different scopes get different instances.

```
builder.RegisterType<MyService>().As<IMyService>().Insta
ncePerDependency();

builder.RegisterType<MySharedService>().As<IMySharedServ
ice>().SingleInstance();

builder.RegisterType<MyScopedService>().As<IMyScopedServ
ice>().InstancePerLifetimeScope();
```

6.5. Engaging Third-Party Libraries

Autofac can also integrate with third-party libraries by providing out-of-the-box utility methods for registration. Let's consider the example of integrating with Log4Net:

```
var builder = new ContainerBuilder();

// Register types
builder.RegisterModule<ServiceModule>();

// Register Log4Net
```

```
builder.Register(c =>
LogManager.GetLogger(typeof(Object))).As<ILog>().SingleI
nstance();

IContainer container = builder.Build();
```

Here, we're asking Autofac to maintain a single instance of the logger throughout the application.

These examples demonstrate the practical side of Autofac, highlighting its versatility and power to handle complex scenarios robustly, yet with enviable ease. Explore different variants and experiment with various configurations to drive maximum advantage from Autofac and Dependency Injection.

Chapter 7. Integrating Autofac with ASP.NET MVC and Web API

In order to integrate Autofac with ASP.NET MVC and Web API, you will first need to install the necessary NuGet packages. In your project, run the following commands: - `Install-Package Autofac` - `Install-Package Autofac.Mvc5` - `Install-Package Autofac.WebApi2`

Once the packages are installed, you'll be able to use Autofac's functionality within your ASP.NET MVC and Web API apps. Autofac provides a special extension for each of these types of applications, which simplifies the integration.

7.1. Setting up the DependencyResolver for MVC

ASP.NET MVC uses a `DependencyResolver` to resolve dependencies of controllers and other components. In order to use Autofac, you'll need to set up a `DependencyResolver` that uses your Autofac `IoC` container. Here is how you can do so:

```
public class MvcApplication : System.Web.HttpApplication
{
    protected void Application_Start() {
        var builder = new ContainerBuilder();

        // Register your MVC controllers.

builder.RegisterControllers(typeof(MvcApplication).Assem
bly);
```

```
        // Set the dependency resolver to be Autofac.
        var container = builder.Build();
        DependencyResolver.SetResolver(new
AutofacDependencyResolver(container));

        // Other MVC config
    }
}
```

When the application starts, it builds an Autofac container and sets the `DependencyResolver` to an instance of `AutofacDependencyResolver` which uses that container.

7.2. Registering MVC Filters

You can use Autofac to inject dependencies into your MVC filters. To enable this, you'll need to register your filters with Autofac in the `Application_Start` method:

```
builder.RegisterFilterProvider();

// If you have custom filters that have dependencies,
don't forget to register them too!
builder.RegisterType<MyCustomFilter>().As<IFilter>().Ins
tancePerRequest();
```

7.3. Setting up the DependencyResolver for Web API

ASP.NET Web API also uses a `DependencyResolver` to resolve dependencies of its controllers. However, it uses a separate interface (`IDependencyResolver`) from the one used by MVC. Autofac provides an extension to set up the Web API `DependencyResolver`:

```
public class WebApiApplication :
System.Web.HttpApplication {
    protected void Application_Start() {
        var builder = new ContainerBuilder();

        // Register your Web API controllers.

builder.RegisterApiControllers(Assembly.GetExecutingAsse
mbly());

        // Set the dependency resolver to be Autofac.
        var container = builder.Build();

GlobalConfiguration.Configuration.DependencyResolver =
            new
AutofacWebApiDependencyResolver(container);

        // Other Web API config
    }
}
```

7.4. Registering Web API Filters

To use Autofac to inject dependencies into your Web API filters, you'll need to perform a specific registration in the `Application_Start` method:

```
builder.RegisterWebApiFilterProvider(GlobalConfiguration
.Configuration);

// If you have custom filters, don't forget to register
them too!
```

```
builder.RegisterType<MyCustomFilter>().AsWebApiAuthoriza
tionFilterFor<ValuesController>().InstancePerRequest();
```

Note: These code samples illustrate the most basic setup. You may need to adjust them to fit your application's specific needs, such as registration of other types, configuration of lifetime scopes, or configuration of modules.

7.5. Shared Registration

If your application uses both MVC and Web API, you can register services that are common for both of them in one place. Just remember, MVC and Web API have separate DependencyResolvers, and you need to set them both. Here is an example of how this can be done:

```
public class Global : System.Web.HttpApplication {
  protected void Application_Start() {
    var builder = new ContainerBuilder();

    // Register common services
    builder.RegisterModule(new
MyCommonServicesModule());

    // Set the MVC dependency resolver.
    var container1 = builder.Build();
    DependencyResolver.SetResolver(new
AutofacDependencyResolver(container1));

    // Set the Web API dependency resolver.
    var container2 = builder.Build();
    GlobalConfiguration.Configuration.DependencyResolver
=
        new AutofacWebApiDependencyResolver(container2);
```

```
      // Other MVC and Web API config
   }
}
```

We've demonstrated the basics of integrating Autofac with ASP.NET MVC and Web API. Remember, your dependency injection setup should be flexible and maintainable. Adjust these examples to your specific needs, and always keep an eye out for improvements.

Chapter 8. Using Autofac with .NET Desktop Applications

There are different approaches and patterns to developing desktop applications in .NET, and each has their particular conditions and peculiarities. Regardless of the specific way you craft your application, utilizing and managing dependencies correctly via Dependency Injection (DI) and, in particular, Autofac, is crucial for clean, maintainable, and testable code. Before we delve into the practical examples, let's have a brief overview of what dependencies are and how Autofac helps manage them.

8.1. Understanding Dependencies in .NET

Dependencies exist in any non-trivial application. Essentially, a dependency is when one component (class, module, function, etc.) of an application relies on another to carry out some operation. For example, let's take a simple case of a CustomerService class that depends on a CustomerRepository class for retrieving customer data from a database.

```
public class CustomerService
{
    private CustomerRepository _customerRepository;

    public CustomerService()
    {
        _customerRepository = new CustomerRepository();
    }
}
```

Here, `CustomerService` is directly dependent on `CustomerRepository`. It's not a problem in and of itself. However, it does make `CustomerService` less flexible. It's hard-wired to `CustomerRepository`, and you can't switch that out independently or put in a mock repository for testing How do we make `CustomerService` more flexible

That's where Dependency Injection (DI) comes in, and Autofac is one of the DI container created to help with managing these dependencies. With DI, we supply (or "inject") dependencies from the outside instead of having the dependent component create them internally.

8.2. How Autofac Works

Autofac works as a container for your dependencies. It controls the lifecycle of the dependencies, creates and disposes of them when necessary. To use Autofac, we need to first register our dependencies with it, and then ask it to build a container for us. We can then ask this container to provide us with instances of the required classes.

The Autofac's container creation is usually done at the application's start-up. It involves several stages:

1. Create an instance of `ContainerBuilder`

2. Register types with the `ContainerBuilder`

3. Call `Build` on the `ContainerBuilder` to create a `IContainer`

8.3. Using Autofac in .NET Desktop Applications

Registering dependencies:

Let's use the previous `CustomerService` and `CustomerRepository` example. First, we must register our classes with Autofac.

```
var builder = new ContainerBuilder();
builder.RegisterType<CustomerRepository>().As<ICustomerR
epository>();
builder.RegisterType<CustomerService>().As<ICustomerServ
ice>();
var container = builder.Build();
```

Here, we're saying that when something needs an ICustomerService,
Autofac should provide an instance of CustomerService.

Resolving dependencies:

Now, to avoid hard-wiring dependencies, instead of CustomerService
creating its own CustomerRepository, we have it passed into the
constructor.

```
public class CustomerService
{
    private ICustomerRepository _customerRepository;

    public CustomerService(ICustomerRepository
customerRepository)
    {
        _customerRepository = customerRepository;
    }
}
```

This is where the power of DI and Autofac comes in. When Autofac
creates a CustomerService object, it sees that CustomerService needs an
ICustomerRepository, looks up what's registered to handle
ICustomerRepository requests, and finds CustomerRepository.

8.4. Implementing Lifetime Scopes

A crucial part of working with desktop applications is managing object lifetimes. Autofac offers a wealth of options, including per-instance, per-request, and single instance. How you control the lifecycle of your dependencies in Autofac, is centered around the concept of 'lifetime scopes'.

Autofac allows developers to decide where and when certain objects should be disposed of. For instance, if an object needs to be created and reused within a certain scope, but not beyond, we can employ a lifetime scope for that.

Using Autofac's lifetime scope features requires you to adopt the disposable pattern in your classes, particularly those interacting with unmanaged resources such as file streams, database connections, etc.

```
public class CustomerDatabase : ICustomerRepository,
IDisposable
{
    //...

    public void Dispose()
    {
        // Close database connection...
    }
}

//...

using (var scope = container.BeginLifetimeScope())
{
    var customerDatabase =
scope.Resolve<ICustomerRepository>();
    // The customerDatabase instance will be disposed
```

```
when the scope ends.
}
```

The versatility of Autofac not just revolves around managing dependencies, doing constructor, property or method injection, but it also allows handling of scenarios where dependencies have dependencies. You'll need to fathom these areas while working on large-scale applications.

8.5. Building Custom Modules

With large projects, instead of writing all your registrations in one place, you might want to spread them out across several classes for better organizational structure. Autofac's solution to this is custom modules.

A custom module is simply a class that inherits from Module. In its Load method, you can put all the registrations that pertain to that module.

```
public class CustomerModule : Module
{
    protected override void Load(ContainerBuilder
builder)
    {

builder.RegisterType<CustomerRepository>().As<ICustomerR
epository>();

builder.RegisterType<CustomerService>().As<ICustomerServ
ice>();
    }
}
```

After you've defined your modules, you can easily register them whilst building your container.

```
var builder = new ContainerBuilder();
builder.RegisterModule<CustomerModule>();
var container = builder.Build();
```

Autofac in .NET Desktop applications, thus allows you to architect a solution that is flexible, scalable and testable. As a .NET developer, understanding and mastering them is fundamental to building quality code and resilient architectures.

Chapter 9. Unit Testing with Autofac: A Recipe for Success

Let's start our journey into the world of Unit Testing with Autofac. A thorough understanding of this topic will undoubtedly elevate your software development skills and allow you to build high-quality, reliable software systems.

9.1. Kick-starting Autofac for Unit Testing

In unit testing, we test individual units of software to verify that they function as expected. To kick-start unit testing with Autofac, you first need to install the Autofac.Extras.Moq or Autofac.Extras.FakeItEasy Nuget package, whichever is your preference.

```
Install-Package Autofac.Extras.Moq
```

or

```
Install-Package Autofac.Extras.FakeItEasy
```

With these packages, Autofac can automatically build your system and provide fakes for dependency injection.

9.2. Understanding Test Initialization

A typical way of initializing these tests involves the use of a 'using' block. This creates an AutoMock, sets up required services, and obtains an instance upon which testing is executed.

```
using (var mock = AutoMock.GetLoose())
{
    mock.Mock<IService>()
      .Setup(x => x.Execute())
      .Returns(expected);

    var cls = mock.Create<Consumer>();

    var actual = cls.UseService();

    Assert.AreEqual(expected, actual);
}
```

In this example, you create a loose AutoMock (any calls for members that aren't set up will return default values). You then set up IService and register it with the mocking framework so it will be provided if requested from your DI container.

9.3. Mastering Fake Services

When working with Autofac, setting up a fake service becomes a walk in the park. You can set up these services and run them directly, resulting in fewer code changes and improved maintainability.

```
using (var mock = AutoMock.GetLoose())
{
  mock.Mock<IService>()
    .Setup(x => x.Execute())
    .Returns(expected);

  var cls = mock.Create<Consumer>();
```

```
    var actual = cls.DoWork();

    Assert.AreEqual(expected, actual);
}
```

The 'DoWork' method manages the method's dependencies behind the scenes. It creates the Consumer object, feeds the fake IService into it, and 'DoWork' calls 'Execute' on IService, which has been set to return our expected result.

9.4. Handling Multiple Services

Autofac's flexibility truly shines when dealing with multiple services. This is frequently seen in complex applications where several dependencies need to be mocked. In such cases, setting up these services with Autofac is seamless and straightforward.

```
using (var mock = AutoMock.GetStrict())
{
  mock.Mock<IService1>()
    .Setup(x => x.Execute())
    .Returns(x);

  mock.Mock<IService2>()
    .Setup(x => x.Execute())
    .Returns(y);

  var cls = mock.Create<MultiConsumer>();

  var actual = cls.DoWork();

  Assert.AreEqual(x + y, actual);
}
```

In this example, 'mock.Create<MultiConsumer>()' sets up both IService1 and IService2 in the MultiConsumer class. You can observe how clean and organized the code is, allowing for easy readability and maintenance.

9.5. Utilizing Strict Mocks

In some cases, you'll need to adopt a stricter approach to your mocking, particularly when you want to ensure your code is interacting with your fakes in a very specific way. For such scenarios, Autofac provides strict mocks.

```
using (var mock = AutoMock.GetStrict())
{
  mock.Mock<IService>()
    .Setup(x => x.Execute())
    .Returns(expected);

  var cls = mock.Create<Consumer>();

  var actual = cls.UseService();

  Assert.AreEqual(expected, actual);
}
```

In this 'strict' mocking methodology, any call that isn't explicitly arranged will throw an exception. This results in very specific and guided unit tests.

9.6. Conclusion

Mastering the art of unit testing with Autofac not only leads to better software design but also substantially enhances the maintainability and reliability of your .NET applications. With the knowledge and practical examples shared in this section, you can start adopting the principles of Autofac in your unit testing strategy today. Remember, the journey of mastering any tool starts with a single step, and the consistent application of learning will compound over time — leading to success in your software development endeavors.

Chapter 10. Troubleshooting Common Issues in Autofac

Autofac, as a potent inversion-of-control (IoC) container, is renowned for delivering high flexibility and adaptability. However, even the best tools can have associated problems and complexities, which is why this chapter is devoted to tackling and troubleshooting common issues that may arise in the process of integrating Autofac in your .NET applications.

10.1. Resolving Component Dependency Issues

One of the primary challenges with Autofac (or any DI Framework) is associated with dependencies among components. This usually manifests as `ComponentNotRegisteredException`, implying that Autofac is incapable of finding a component's dependency in its container.

The most direct solution is to ensure dependencies are registered before any attempt to resolve a component. A proper sequence should be adhered to: Register → Build → Begin Scope → Resolve.

```
var builder = new ContainerBuilder();
builder.RegisterType<MyComponent>();
var container = builder.Build();
using(var scope = container.BeginLifetimeScope())
{
    var myComponent = scope.Resolve<MyComponent>();
}
```

Remember, Autofac adopts a late-bound style of configuration. As such, an issue with configuration doesn't become apparent until you

39

try to resolve the component.

10.2. Incorrect Lifetimes Hindering Efficiency

Autofac provides different lifetime scopes (i.e., `InstancePerDependency`, `SingleInstance`, `InstancePerLifetimeScope`) to control components' scopes. Misusing these can lead to efficiency issues or even side effects.

For instance, if a `SingleInstance` component has a dependency on `InstancePerDependency` or `InstancePerLifetimeScope` component, every time the single instance component gets resolved, the dependency gets re-resolved too. This practice, particularly with SingleInstance components having a sizable state or requiring extensive resources for instantiation, can lead to an unforeseen performance hit.

The key to mitigating this is understanding each component's nature and how often it gets used. This understanding will directly impact the efficiency of the application.

10.3. ContainerBuilder Update Misuse

In previous versions of Autofac (pre-4.0), `ContainerBuilder.Update(container)` was used commonly to add registrations to an already built container. However, this method became obsolete because of the associated potential threading issues.

Many developers still find themselves stuck with massive legacy codebases that use this outlawed method. Autofac recommends switching to `ContainerBuilder.Build()` method, used post original container creation to build a new container that includes the extra components.

In conclusion, even though the changes might be on the heavier side, replacing `Update()` with `Build()` will prove beneficially healthy for your application in the long run.

10.4. Understanding 'No Parameterless Constructor Defined' Exception

This .NET exception is thrown when Autofac tries to create an instance of a class without a parameterless constructor. A common mistake is forgetting to register a class with Autofac that's being used as a constructor parameter in another class.

```
public class MyClass
{
    public MyClass(DependencyClass dependency)
    {
        //...
    }
}
```

In the above code, if `DependencyClass` isn't registered with Autofac, then it throws an exception while trying to create an instance of `MyClass`.

The solution is to ensure all dependencies are registered with Autofac before resolving dependent classes.

10.5. Not Disposing of Lifetime Scopes

One of the most common issues causing memory leaks is the failure to dispose of lifetime scopes after using them. Failing to do so keeps all the resolved component instances in the memory.

```
var scope = container.BeginLifetimeScope();
```

Perform operations in the scope (usually a using statement), which automatically disposes it when execution goes out of the block.

```
using(var scope = container.BeginLifetimeScope())
{
    //operations
}
```

In conclusion, Autofac is a powerful tool but requires thorough knowledge for effective usage. Understanding and troubleshooting common issues will go a long way in utilizing its potential and avoiding pitfalls, thus enabling you to architect scalable and loosely-coupled .NET applications.

Chapter 11. Best Practices: Leveraging the Full Potential of Autofac

As one delves deeper into the utilities of Autofac, it is essential to identify and implement best practices, so as to fully benefit from this powerful tool. These practices promote cleanly written, maintainable, and scalable code. This chapter provides an exposition of such practices, along with practical examples and guidelines.

11.1. Embrace Constructor Injection

The Constructor Injection design pattern should be the preferred choice when implementing dependency injection with Autofac. By offloading the task of handling dependencies to the constructor, the classes become loosely coupled and well-organized.

```
public class MyClass
{
   private IMyDependency _dependency;

   public MyClass(IMyDependency dependency)
   {
     _dependency = dependency;
   }
}
```

Here, MyClass depends on an instance of IMyDependency that's supplied via the constructor.

11.2. Avoid Service Locator

In the context of Dependency Injection, using Service Locator is often viewed as an anti-pattern. It can make your code hard to understand and maintain over time. Relying on the Container to resolve dependencies should be your last resort.

11.3. Apply Module Registrations

Autofac Modules allow you to encapsulate a set of related dependencies into a reusable unit. They enforce better organization and make dependency tracking easier. Use Modules to split your registrations into logical groups.

```csharp
public class InfrastructureModule : Module
{
    protected override void Load(ContainerBuilder builder)
    {

builder.RegisterType<MyService>().As<IMyService>();
    }
}
```

11.4. Leverage Lifetime Scopes

Lifetime scopes are an extraordinary feature of Autofac that allow you to manage when instances are shared or created new.

- Per Dependency: A new instance is created every time a dependency is requested.

- Single Instance: Only one instance is created, and the same instance is used whenever the dependency is required.

- Instance Per Lifetime Scope: A new instance is created once per scope.

Leveraging lifetime scopes can vastly improve your ability to manage resources especially in applications with many transient and singleton services.

11.5. Use AsImplementedInterfaces for Interface Registrations

If your classes are implementing multiple interfaces, you can utilize the `AsImplementedInterfaces()` method for concise and clean registration.

```
public class MyService : IServiceA, IServiceB

containerBuilder.Register(c => new
MyService()).AsImplementedInterfaces();
```

11.6. Use Property and Method Injection Sparingly

While property and method injection provide additional layers of flexibility, they should be used sparingly due to their implicit nature. Be disciplined and limit their use to cases which constructor injection can't handle.

11.7. Factor in Assembly Scanning

Autofac allows assembly scanning feature to register types in bulk. This approach is quite beneficial in large applications where manual registrations can become overwhelming.

```
builder.RegisterAssemblyTypes(AppDomain.CurrentDomain.Ge
tAssemblies())
        .Where(t => t.Name.EndsWith("Service"))
        .AsImplementedInterfaces();
```

11.8. Opt for Delegate Factories

Instead of laboriously resolving dependencies using Func<T> delegate, you can define a delegate factory that provides a more transparent and intuitive way of creating instances.

```
public delegate IMyClass MyClassFactory(int parameter);

builder.RegisterType<MyClass>().AsSelf();
```

In the example above, MyClassFactory is a delegate that represents a factory for creating IMyClass objects. Autofac automatically implements this factory pattern.

Remember, Autofac is an extremely potent tool, which when used correctly can significantly enhance the quality and maintainability of your code base. It might take some time to familiarize yourself with its many features and conventions, but the reward is well-worth the investment.